---

## YOU LEFT ME, SWEETS, TWO LEGACIES

---

FAMOUS LOVE POEMS

*COMPILED BY*

AVIRA N

CLASSIC BOOKS

First published by Classic Books in 2017

Copyright © Avira N, 2017

All rights reserved. This book is licensed for your personal enjoyment only. It is illegal to copy this book, post it to a website, or distribute it by any other means without permission. This book may not be re-sold or given away to other people.

Cover Design: Classic Books

Classic Books, 2017

First Edition

ISBN: 978-1-7751580-1-1

## PREFACE

Poetry's origin can be traced way back before literacy came into light. The ancient civilizations all around the world used oral poetry to convey their traditions and to keep a record of their history. The epic poems are a fine example of ancient form of poetry.

The Divine Comedy (1308 – 1320)

"All my thoughts always speak to me of love,

Yet have between themselves such difference

That while one bids me bow with mind and sense,

A second saith, 'Go to: look thou above';

The third one, hoping, yields me joy enough;

And with the last come tears, I scarce know whence:

All of them craving pity in sore suspense,

Trembling with fears that the heart knoweth of.

And thus, being all unsure which path to take,

Wishing to speak I know not what to say,

And lose myself in amorous wanderings:

Until (my peace with all of them to make),

Unto mine enemy I needs must pray,

My lady Pity, for the help she brings."


With advanced techniques in writing, poetry became more of an organised approach with advanced format, use of metaphors, similes, resonance, and free verse. In poetry, we look for the musical metre, the recurrent refrain of rhythm; while that which inspires it arises from the universal motives which Coleridge names as ministers to Love.


"All thoughts, all passions, all delights, Whatever stirs this mortal frame."


And Poetry's outstanding mission is to unite love and truth together.

"Loving in truth, and fain in verse my love to show,

That she, dear she, might take some pleasure of my pain,—

Pleasure might cause her read, reading might make her know,

Knowledge might pity win, and pity grace obtain,"

(Sir Philip Sidney)


"love is more thicker than forget

more thinner than recall

more seldom than a wave is wet

more frequent than to fail"

(E E Cummings)


William Shakespeare's Sonnet 147 throws light on consuming nature of love.


My love is as a fever, longing still

For that which longer nurseth the disease,

Feeding on that which doth preserve the ill,

Th' uncertain sickly appetite to please.

My reason, the physician to my love,

Angry that his prescriptions are not kept,

Hath left me, and I desperate now approve

Desire is death, which physic did except.

Past cure I am, now reason is past care,

And frantic-mad with evermore unrest;

My thoughts and my discourse as madmen's are,

At random from the truth vainly expressed:

For I have sworn thee fair, and thought thee bright,

Who art as black as hell, as dark as night.


But then, love, as we all know, is a two-sided thing; with the joy there comes the pain.


"The hottest love has the coldest end." - Socrates


Whereas the joy in love comes as a swift flowing river, pain when arrives is always more intense, more unbearable, and sharper - the river of joy comes firs, and then follows the vast ocean of pain. The pain with time diminishes to a ghost, but when it is there, it is one great suffering - greater than the joy love brings. The Poets, by the very necessity of their vocation, are the closest students of language in any literature. They are the most exacting in their demands upon the resources of words, and the most careful of discriminations in their use. Famous poets of all the times, from all around the world have used poetry to explore this powerful emotion of love. In *YOU left me, sweets, two legacies*, I have included poems that deal with both sides of love.

The title of this book "YOU left me, sweets, two legacies" is taken from Emily Dickinson's poem "YOU left me, sweet, two legacies" in which she presented two sides of love.

YOU left me, sweet, two legacies,—

A legacy of love

A Heavenly Father would content,

Had He the offer of;


You left me boundaries of pain

Capacious as the sea,

Between eternity and time,

Your consciousness and me.

The first half of the poem discusses the joyful side of love – the love is so large and immense that even God himself would happily take the offer if given. In the second half of the poem, Dickinson presented the readers with view of insupportable loneliness after the love is lost. The void, the large hole of pain, the speaker felt after the lover has left, is compared to girth of the sea.

My objective in *YOU left me, sweets two legacies* is to offer the reader with some of the most famous classic poets' work known for their poignant lines on love. In search of the best love poems, I have taken work of several poets including Emily Dickinson, Christina Rossetti, E E Cummings, Sara Teasdale, Amy Lowell, Robert Browning, John Clare, Percy Bysshe Shelley, Ella Wheeler Wilcox, and Elizabeth Barrett Browning ordering them haphazardly. Finally, an explanation about my role as compiler of this book. This is not a critical edition of all the above-mentioned poets' work. I do not intend this collection to be regarded as the one. I have kept the poets' unique style; the peculiar use of punctuation and capitalisation that may seem out of place to a more modern reader: E.E. Cummings, for example, deliberately abandoned conventional syntax in nearly all of his poems. My goal is just to present readers with a collection of some of the best poetic work of influential poets of all times.

Avira N

## LOVE IS MORE THICKER THAN FORGET

love is more thicker than forget

more thinner than recall

more seldom than a wave is wet

more frequent than to fail


it is most mad and moonly

and less it shall unbe

than all the sea which only

is deeper than the sea


love is less always than to win

less never than alive

less bigger than the least begin

less littler than forgive

it is most sane and sunly

and more it cannot die

than all the sky which only

is higher than the sky

-E E Cummings

## HEART, WE WILL FORGET HIM

HEART, we will forget him!
 You and I, to-night!
You may forget the warmth he gave,
I will forget the light.

When you have done, pray tell me,
   That I my thoughts may dim;
 Haste! lest while you're lagging,
I may remember him!

–Emily Dickinson

## BURIED LOVE

I have come to bury Love

Beneath a tree,

In the forest tall and black

Where none can see.

I shall put no flowers at his head,

Nor stone at his feet,

For the mouth I loved so much

Was bittersweet.

I shall go no more to his grave,

For the woods are cold.

I shall gather as much of joy

As my hands can hold.

I shall stay all day in the sun

Where the wide winds blow,—

But oh, I shall cry at night

When none will know.

- Sara Teasdale

## I AM NOT YOURS

I am not yours, not lost in you,

Not lost, although I long to be

Lost as a candle lit at noon,

Lost as a snowflake in the sea.

You love me, and I find you still

A spirit beautiful and bright,

Yet I am I, who long to be

Lost as a light is lost in light.

Oh plunge me deep in love—put out

My senses, leave me deaf and blind,

Swept by the tempest of your love,

A taper in a rushing wind.

-Sara Teasdale

# I LOVED YOU FIRST

I loved you first: but afterwards your love

Outsoaring mine, sang such a loftier song

As drowned the friendly cooings of my dove.

Which owes the other most? my love was long, And

yours one moment seemed to wax more strong; I

loved and guessed at you, you construed me

And loved me for what might or might not be –

Nay, weights and measures do us both a wrong. For

verily love knows not 'mine' or 'thine;'

With separate 'I' and 'thou' free love has done, For

one is both and both are one in love:

Rich love knows nought of 'thine that is not mine;'

Both have the strength and both the length thereof,

Both of us, of the love which makes us one.

-Christina Rossetti

## If THOU MUST LOVE ME

If thou must love me, let it be for nought

Except for love's sake only. Do not say

I love her for her smile ... her look ... her way

Of speaking gently, ... for a trick of thought

That falls in well with mine, and certes brought

A sense of pleasant ease on such a day'—

For these things in themselves, Beloved, may

Be changed, or change for thee,—and love, so wrought,

May be unwrought so. Neither love me for

Thine own dear pity's wiping my cheeks dry,—

A creature might forget to weep, who bore

Thy comfort long, and lose thy love thereby!

But love me for love's sake, that evermore

Thou may'st love on, through love's eternity.

-Elizabeth Barrett Browning

## SOMEWHERE I HAVE NEVER TRAVELLED

somewhere i have never travelled, gladly beyond

any experience, your eyes have their silence:

in your most frail gesture are things which enclose me,

or which i cannot touch because they are too near


your slightest look easily will unclose me

though i have closed myself as fingers,

you open always petal by petal myself as Spring opens

(touching skilfully, mysteriously) her first rose


or if your wish be to close me, i and

my life will shut very beautifully, suddenly,

as when the heart of this flower imagines

the snow carefully everywhere descending;


nothing which we are to perceive in this world equals

the power of your intense fragility: whose texture

compels me with the colour of its countries,

rendering death and forever with each breathing

(i do not know what it is about you that closes

and opens; only something in me understands

the voice of your eyes is deeper than all roses)

nobody, not even the rain, has such small hands

-E E Cummings

# CONFLUENTS

As rivers seek the sea,

Much more deep than they,

So my soul seeks thee

Far away:

As running rivers moan

On their course alone

So I moan

Left alone.


As the delicate rose

To the sun's sweet strength

Doth herself unclose,

Breadth and length:

So spreads my heart to thee

Unveiled utterly,

I to thee

Utterly.

As morning dew exhales

Sunwards pure and free,

So my spirit fails

After thee:

As dew leaves not a trace

On the green earth's face;

I, no trace

On thy face.


Its goal the river knows,

Dewdrops find a way,

Sunlight cheers the rose

In her day:

Shall I, lone sorrow past,

Find thee at the last?

Sorrow past,

Thee at last?

-Christina Rossetti

## MIRAGE

How is it that, being gone, you fill my days,

And all the long nights are made glad by thee?

No loneliness is this, nor misery,

But great content that these should be the ways

Whereby the Fancy, dreaming as she strays,

Makes bright and present what she would would be.

And who shall say if the reality

Is not with dreams so pregnant.  For delays

And hindrances may bar the wished-for end;

A thousand misconceptions may prevent

Our souls from coming near enough to blend;

Let me but think we have the same intent,

That each one needs to call the other, "friend!"

It may be vain illusion.  I'm content.

-Amy Lowell

## I LIKE MY BODY WHEN IT IS WITH

i like my body when it is with your

body. It is so quite new a thing.

Muscles better and nerves more.

i like your body, i like what it does,

i like its hows, i like to feel the spine

of your body and its bones, and the trembling

-firm-smooth ness and which i will

again and again and again

kiss, i like kissing this and that of you,

i like, slowly stroking the, shocking fuzz

of your electric fur, and what-is-it comes

over parting flesh .... And eyes big love-crumbs,

and possibly i like the thrill

of under me you so quite new

-E E Cummings

## IF THERE ARE ANY HEAVENS

if there are any heavens my mother will (all by herself
)have

one. It will not be a pansy heaven nor

a fragile heaven of lilies-of-the-valley but

it will be a heaven of blackred roses

my father will be (deep like a rose

tall like a rose)

standing near my

(swaying over her

silent)

with eyes which are really petals and see

nothing with the face of a poet really which

is a flower and not a face with

hands

which whisper

This is my beloved my

(suddenly in sunlight

he will bow,

& the whole garden will bow)

-E E Cummings

## YOU'LL LOVE ME YET

YOU'LL love me yet!—and I can tarry

Your love's protracted growing:

June rear'd that bunch of flowers you carry,

From seeds of April's sowing.


I plant a heartful now: some seed

At least is sure to strike,

And yield—what you'll not pluck indeed,

Not love, but, may be, like.


You'll look at least on love's remains,

A grave's one violet:

Your look?—that pays a thousand pains.

What's death? You'll love me yet!

-Robert Browning

## IT 'S ALL I HAVE TO BRING TODAY

IT 'S all I have to bring to-day,

This, and my heart beside,

This, and my heart, and all the fields,

And all the meadows wide.

Be sure you count, should I forget,—

Some one the sun could tell,—

This, and my heart, and all the bees

Which in the clover dwell.

-Emily Dickinson

## LOVE IS ANTERIOR TO LIFE

LOVE is anterior to life,

Posterior to death,

Initial of creation, and

The exponent of breath.

-Emily Dickinson

## YOU LEFT ME SWEET TWO LEGACIES

YOU left me, sweet, two legacies,—

A legacy of love

A Heavenly Father would content,

Had He the offer of;

You left me boundaries of pain

Capacious as the sea,

Between eternity and time,

Your consciousness and me.

-Emily Dickinson

## IT MAY NOT BE ALWAYS BE SO

it may not always be so; and i say

that if your lips, which i have loved, should touch

another's, and your dear strong fingers clutch

his heart, as mine in time not far away;

if on another's face your sweet hair lay

in such a silence as i know, or such

great writhing words as, uttering overmuch,

stand helplessly before the spirit at bay;

if this should be, i say if this should be

you of my heart, send me a little word;

that i may go unto him, and take his hands,

saying, Accept all happiness from me.

Then shall i turn my face, and hear one bird

sing terribly afar in the lost lands.

-E E Cummings

## MAY

I cannot tell you how it was;

But this I know: it came to pass

Upon a bright and breezy day

When May was young; ah, pleasant May!

As yet the poppies were not born

Between the blades of tender corn;

The last eggs had not hatched as yet,

Nor any bird foregone its mate.

I cannot tell you what it was;

But this I know: it did but pass.

It passed away with sunny May,

With all sweet things it passed away,

And left me old, and cold, and gray.

-Christina Rossetti

## IF YOU WERE COMING IN THE FALL

IF you were coming in the fall,
I 'd brush the summer by
With half a smile and half a spurn,
As housewives do a fly.

If I could see you in a year,
I 'd wind the months in balls,
And put them each in separate drawers,
Until their time befalls.

If only centuries delayed,
I 'd count them on my hand,
Subtracting till my fingers dropped
Into Van Diemen's land.

If certain, when this life was out,
That yours and mine should be,

I 'd toss it yonder like a rind,

And taste eternity.


But now, all ignorant of the length

Of time's uncertain wing,

It goads me, like the goblin bee,

That will not state its sting.

-Emily Dickinson

## A BIRTHDAY

My heart is like a singing bird

Whose nest is in a watered shoot;

My heart is like an apple-tree

Whose boughs are bent with thickset fruit;

My heart is like a rainbow shell

That paddles in a halcyon sea;

My heart is gladder than all these,

Because my love is come to me.

-Christina Rossetti

## HE TOUCHED ME SO I LIVE TO KNOW

HE touched me, so I live to know

That such a day, permitted so,

I groped upon his breast.

It was a boundless place to me,

And silenced, as the awful sea

Puts minor streams to rest.


And now, I 'm different from before,

As if I breathed superior air,

Or brushed a royal gown;

My feet, too, that had wandered so,

My gypsy face transfigured now

To tenderer renown.

-Emily Dickinson

## THE MOON IS DISTANCE FROM THE SEA

THE MOON is distant from the sea,
And yet with amber hands
She leads him, docile as a boy,
Along appointed sands.

He never misses a degree;
Obedient to her eye,
He comes just so far toward the town,
Just so far goes away.

Oh, Signor, thine the amber hand,
And mine the distant sea,—
Obedient to the least command
Thine eyes impose on me.

-Emily Dickinson

## I WISH I COULD REMEMBER

I wish I could remember that first day,

First hour, first moment of your meeting me,

If bright or dim the season, it might be

Summer or Winter for aught I can say;

So unrecorded did it slip away,

So blind was I to see and to foresee,

So dull to mark the budding of my tree

That would not blossom for many a May.

If only I could recollect it, such

A day of days! I let it come and go

As traceless as a thaw of bygone snow;

It seemed to mean so little, meant so much;

If only now I could recall that touch,

First touch of hand in hand—Did one but know!

-Christina Rossetti

## CROWNED

You came to me bearing bright roses,

Red like the wine of your heart;

You twisted them into a garland

To set me aside from the mart.

Red roses to crown me your lover,

And I walked aureoled and apart.

Enslaved and encircled, I bore it,

Proud token of my gift to you.

The petals waned paler, and shriveled,

And dropped; and the thorns started through.

Bitter thorns to proclaim me your lover,

A diadem woven with rue.

-Amy Lowell

## SONG

She sat and sang alway

By the green margin of a stream,

Watching the fishes leap and play

Beneath the glad sunbeam.


I sat and wept alway

Beneath the moon's most shadowy beam,

Watching the blossoms of the May

Weep leaves into the stream.


I wept for memory;

She sang for hope that is so fair:

My tears were swallowed by the sea;

Her songs died on the air.

-Christina Rossetti

## THAT I DID ALWAYS LOVE

THAT I did always love,

I bring thee proof:

That till I loved

I did not love enough.

That I shall love always,

I offer thee

That love is life,

And life hath immortality.

This, dost thou doubt, sweet?

Then have I

Nothing to show

But Calvary.

-Emily Dickinson

## NOT WITH A CLUB THE HEART IS BROKEN

NOT with a club the heart is broken,

Nor with a stone;

A whip, so small you could not see it,

I 've known

To lash the magic creature

Till it fell,

Yet that whip's name too noble

Then to tell.

Magnanimous of bird

By boy descried,

To sing unto the stone

Of which it died.

-Emily Dickinson

## WHEN ROSES CEASE TO BLOOM

WHEN roses cease to bloom, dear,

And violets are done,

When bumble-bees in solemn flight

Have passed beyond the sun,

The hand that paused to gather

Upon this summer's day

Will idle lie, in Auburn,—

Then take my flower, pray!

-Emily Dickinson

## SONNET 43

How do I love thee? Let me count the ways.

I love thee to the depth and breadth and height

My soul can reach, when feeling out of sight

For the ends of being and ideal grace.

I love thee to the level of every day's

Most quiet need, by sun and candle-light.

I love thee freely, as men strive for right.

I love thee purely, as they turn from praise.

I love thee with the passion put to use

In my old griefs, and with my childhood's faith.

I love thee with a love I seemed to lose

With my lost saints. I love thee with the breath,

Smiles, tears, of all my life; and, if God choose,

I shall but love thee better after death.

-Elizabeth Barrett Browning

## WE OUTGROW LOVE LIKE OTHER THINGS

WE outgrow love like other things

And put it in the drawer,

Till it an antique fashion shows

Like costumes grandsires wore.

-Emily Dickionson

## NIGHT SONG AT AMALFI

I asked the heaven of stars

What I should give my love—

It answered me with silence,

Silence above.

I asked the darkened sea

Down where the fishers go—

It answered me with silence,

Silence below.

Oh, I could give him weeping,

Or I could give him song—

But how can I give silence,

My whole life long?

-Sara Teasdale

## I CARRY YOUR HEART WITH ME

i carry your heart with me (i carry it in

my heart) i am never without it(anywhere

i go you go,my dear;and whatever is done

by only me is your doing,my darling)


i fear

no fate (for you are my fate,my sweet) i want

no world (for beautiful you are my world,my true)

and it's you are whatever a moon has always meant

and whatever a sun will always sing is you

here is the deepest secret nobody knows

(here is the root of the root and the bud of the bud

and the sky of the sky of a tree called life; which grows

higher than soul can hope or mind can hide)

and this is the wonder that's keeping the stars apart

i carry your heart (i carry it in my heart)

-E E Cummings

## THE WAY I READ A LETTER IS THIS

THE WAY I read a letter's this:

'T is first I lock the door,

And push it with my fingers next,

For transport it be sure.


And then I go the furthest off

To counteract a knock;

Then draw my little letter forth

And softly pick its lock.


Then, glancing narrow at the wall,

And narrow at the floor,

For firm conviction of a mouse

Not exorcised before,


Peruse how infinite I am

To—no one that you know!

And sigh for lack of heaven,—but not

The heaven the creeds bestow.

-Emily Dickinson

## THE LOOK

Stephon kissed me in the spring,

Robin in the fall,

But Colin only looked at me

And never kissed at all.

Strephon's kiss was lost in jest,

Robin's lost in play,

But the kiss in Colin's eyes

Haunts me night and day.

-Sara Teasdale

## GIFTS

I gave my first love laughter,

I gave my second tears,

I gave my third love silence

Through all the years.

My first love gave me singing,

My second eyes to see,

But oh, it was my third love

Who gave my soul to me.

-Sara Teasdale

## WILD ASTERS

In the spring I asked the daisies

If his words were true,

And the clever, clear-eyed daisies

Always knew.

Now the fields are brown and barren,

Bitter autumn blows,

And of all the stupid asters

Not one knows.

-Sara Teasdale

## DEBT

What do I owe to you

Who loved me deep and long?

You never gave my spirit wings

Or gave my heart a song.

But oh, to him I loved,

Who loved me not at all,

I owe the open gate

That led through heaven's wall.

-Sara Teasdale

## I SHALL NOT CARE

When I am dead and over me bright April

Shakes out her rain-drenched hair,

Though you should lean above me broken-hearted,

I shall not care.

I shall have peace, as leafy trees are peaceful

When rain bends down the bough,

And I shall be more silent and cold-hearted

Than you are now.

-Sara Teasdale

## LOVE FROM THE NORTH

I had a love in soft south land,

Beloved through April far in May;

He waited on my lightest breath,

And never dared to say me nay.

He saddened if my cheer was sad,

But gay he grew if I was gay;

We never differed on a hair,

My yes his yes, my nay his nay.

The wedding hour was come, the aisles

Were flushed with sun and flowers that day;

pacing balanced in my thoughts,--

"It's quite too late to think of nay."--

My bridegroom answered in his turn,

Myself had almost answered "yea":

When through the flashing nave I heard.
A struggle and resounding "nay."

Bridemaids and bridegroom shrank in fear,
But I stood high who stood at bay:
"And if I answer yea, fair Sir,
What man art thou to bar with nay?"

He was a strong man from the north,
Light-locked, with eyes of dangerous gray:
"Put yea by for another time
In which I will not say thee nay."

He took me in his strong white arms,
He bore me on his horse away
O'er crag, morass, and hair-breadth pass,
But never asked me yea or nay.

He made me fast with book and bell,

With links of love he makes me stay;

Till now I've neither heart nor power

Nor will nor wish to say him nay.

-Christina Rossetti

## AFTER PARTING

Oh, I have sown my love so wide
That he will find it everywhere;
It will awake him in the night,
It will enfold him in the air.

I set my shadow in his sight
And I have winged it with desire,
That it may be a cloud by day,
And in the night a shaft of fire.
-Sara Teasdale

## TIDES

Love in my heart was a fresh tide flowing

Where the starlike sea gulls soar;

The sun was keen and the foam was blowing

High on the rocky shore.

But now in the dusk the tide is turning,

Lower the sea gulls soar,

And the waves that rose in resistless yearning

Are broken forevermore.

-Sara Teasdale

## SWANS

Night is over the park, and a few brave stars
Look on the lights that link it with chains of gold,
The lake bears up their reflection in broken bars
That seem too heavy for tremulous water to hold.

We watch the swans that sleep in a shadowy place,
And now and again one wakes and uplifts its head;
How still you are—your gaze is on my face—
We watch the swans and never a word is said.

-Sara Teasdale

## I WOULD LIVE IN YOUR LOVE

I would live in your love

as the sea-grasses live in the sea,

Borne up by each wave as it passes,

drawn down by each wave that recedes;

I would empty my soul of the dreams

that have gathered in me,

I would beat with your heart as it beats,

I would follow your soul as it leads.

-Sara Teasdale

## WHEN I AM DEAD

When I am dead, my dearest,

Sing no sad songs for me;

Plant thou no roses at my head,

Nor shady cypress tree:

Be the green grass above me

With showers and dewdrops wet;

And if thou wilt, remember,

And if thou wilt, forget.


I shall not see the shadows,

I shall not feel the rain;

I shall not hear the nightingale

Sing on, as if in pain:

And dreaming through the twilight

That doth not rise nor set,

Haply I may remember,

And haply may forget.

-Christina Rossetti

## REMEMBER

Remember me when I am gone away,

Gone far away into the silent land;

When you can no more hold me by the hand,

Nor I half turn to go yet turning stay.

Remember me when no more day by day

You tell me of our future that you plann'd:

Only remember me; you understand

It will be late to counsel then or pray.

Yet if you should forget me for a while

And afterwards remember, do not grieve:

For if the darkness and corruption leave

A vestige of the thoughts that once I had,

Better by far you should forget and smile

Than that you should remember and be sad.

-Christina Rossetti

# GROWN AND FLOWN

I loved my love from green of Spring
 Until sere Autumn's fall;
 But now that leaves are withering
 How should one love at all?
 One heart's too small
 For hunger, cold, love, everything.

I loved my love on sunny days
Until late Summer's wane;
But now that frost begins to glaze
How should one love again? 10
Nay, love and pain
Walk wide apart in diverse ways.

I loved my love—alas to see
That this should be, alas!

I thought that this could scarcely be,

Yet has it come to pass:

Sweet sweet love was,

Now bitter bitter grown to me.

-Christina Rossetti

## THE GHOSTS

I went back to the clanging city,
I went back where my old loves stayed,
But my heart was full of my new love's glory,
My eyes were laughing and unafraid.

I met one who had loved me madly
And told his love for all to hear—
But we talked of a thousand things together,
The past was buried too deep to fear.

I met the other, whose love was given
With never a kiss and scarcely a word—
Oh, it was then the terror took me
Of words unuttered that breathed and stirred.

Oh, love that lives its life with laughter

Or love that lives its life with tears

Can die—but love that is never spoken

Goes like a ghost through the winding years. . . .

I went back to the clanging city,

I went back where my old loves stayed,

My heart was full of my new love's glory,—

But my eyes were suddenly afraid.

-Sara Teasdale

## NEW LOVE AND OLD

In my heart the old love

Struggled with the new;

It was ghostly waking

All night through.


Dear things, kind things,

That my old love said,

Ranged themselves reproachfully

Round my bed.


But I could not heed them,

For I seemed to see

The eyes of my new love

Fixed on me.


Old love, old love,

How can I be true?

Shall I be faithless to myself

Or to you?

-Sara Teasdale

## AFTER LOVE

There is no magic any more,

We meet as other people do,

You work no miracle for me

Nor I for you.

You were the wind and I the sea—

There is no splendor any more,

I have grown listless as the pool

Beside the shore.

But though the pool is safe from storm

And from the tide has found surcease,

It grows more bitter than the sea,

For all its peace.

-Sara Teasdale

## MAY WIND

I said, "I have shut my heart
As one shuts an open door,
That Love may starve therein
And trouble me no more."

But over the roofs there came
The wet new wind of May,
And a tune blew up from the curb
Where the street-pianos play.

My room was white with the sun
And Love cried out in me,
"I am strong, I will break your heart
Unless you set me free."

-Sara Teasdale

## A PRAYER

Until I lose my soul and lie

Blind to the beauty of the earth,

Deaf though shouting wind goes by,

Dumb in a storm of mirth;

Until my heart is quenched at length

And I have left the land of men,

Oh, let me love with all my strength

Careless if I am loved again.

-Sara Teasdale

## THE SONG FOR COLIN

I sang a song at dusking time

Beneath the evening star,

And Terence left his latest rhyme

To answer from afar.


Pierrot laid down his lute to weep,

And sighed, "She sings for me."

But Colin slept a careless sleep

Beneath an apple tree.

-Sara Teasdale

## COMMUNISM

When my blood flows calm as a purling river,

When my heart is asleep and my brain has sway,

It is then that I vow we must part forever,

That I will forget you, and put you away

Out of my life, as a dream is banished

Out of the mind when the dreamer awakes;

That I know it will be, when the spell has vanished,

Better for both of our sakes.


When the court of the mind is ruled by Reason,

I know it is wiser for us to part;

But Love is a spy who is plotting treason,

In league with that warm, red rebel, the Heart.

They whisper to me that the King is cruel,

That his reign is wicked, his law a sin;

And every word they utter is fuel

To the flame that smoulders within.

And on nights like this, when my blood runs riot
With the fever of youth and its mad desires,
When my brain in vain bids my heart be quiet,
When my breast seems the centre of lava-fires,
Oh, then is the time when most I miss you,
And I swear by the stars and my soul and say
That I will have you and hold you and kiss you,
Though the whole world stands in the way.

And like Communists, as mad, as disloyal,
My fierce emotions roam out of their lair;
They hate King Reason for being royal;
They would fire his castle, and burn him there.
Oh, Love! they would clasp you and crush you and kill you,
In the insurrection of uncontrol.
Across the miles, does this wild war thrill you

That is raging in my soul?

-Ella Wheeler Wilcox

## MUSIC WHEN SOFT VOICES DIE

Music, when soft voices die,

Vibrates in the memory -

Odours, when sweet violets sicken,

Live within the sense they quicken.

Rose leaves, when the rose is dead,

Are heap'd for the belovèd's bed;

And so thy thoughts, when thou art gone,

Love itself shall slumber on.

-Percy Bysshe Shelley

## AN END

Love, strong as Death, is dead.

Come, let us make his bed

Among the dying flowers:

A green turf at his head;

And a stone at his feet,

Whereon we may sit

In the quiet evening hours.


He was born in the Spring,

And died before the harvesting:

On the last warm summer day

He left us; he would not stay

For autumn twilight, cold and gray.

Sit we by his grave, and sing

He is gone away.

To few chords and sad and low

Sing we so:

Be our eyes fixed on the grass

Shadow-veiled as the years pass,

While we think of all that was

In the long ago.

-Christina Rossetti

## THE ROSE AND THE BEE

IF I were a bee and you were a rose,

Would you let me in when the gray wind blows?

Would you hold your petals wide apart,

Would you let me in to find your heart,

If you were a rose?

"If I were a rose and you were a bee,

You should never go when you came to me,

I should hold my love on my heart at last,

I should close my leaves and keep you fast,

If you were a bee."

-Sara Teasdale

## SPRING

IN Central Park the lovers sit,

On every hilly path they stroll,

Each thinks his love is infinite,

And crowns his soul.


But we are cynical and wise,

We walk a careful foot apart,

You make a little joke that tries

To hide your heart.


Give over, we have laughed enough;

Oh dearest and most foolish friend,

Why do you wage a war with love

To lose your battle in the end?

-Sara Teasdale

## THE MEETING

HERE we meet, too soon to part,

Here to leave will raise a smart,

Here I'll press thee to my heart,

Where none have place above thee:

Here I vow to love thee well,

And could words unseal the spell,

Had but language strength to tell,

I'd say how much I love thee.


Here, the rose that decks thy door,

Here, the thorn that spreads thy bow'r,

Here, the willow on the moor,

The birds at rest above thee,

Had they light of life to see,

Sense of soul like thee and me,

Soon might each a witness be

How doatingly I love thee.

By the night-sky's purple ether,

And by even's sweetest weather,

That oft has blest us both together,—

The moon that shines above thee,

And shews thy beauteous cheek so blooming,

And by pale age's winter coming,

The charms, and casualties of woman,

I will for ever love thee.

-John Clare

## A GIFT

See!  I give myself to you, Beloved!

My words are little jars

For you to take and put upon a shelf.

Their shapes are quaint and beautiful,

And they have many pleasant colours and lustres

To recommend them.

Also the scent from them fills the room

With sweetness of flowers and crushed grasses.


When I shall have given you the last one,

You will have the whole of me,

But I shall be dead.

-Amy Lowell

## LET IT BE FORGOTTEN

Let it be forgotten, as a flower is forgotten,

Forgotten as a fire that once was singing

gold, Let it be forgotten forever and ever,

Time is a kind friend, he will make us old.

If anyone asks, say it was forgotten

Long and long ago,

As a flower, as a fire, as a hushed footfall In a

long-forgotten snow.

-Sara Teasdale

## AFTER DEATH.

The curtains were half drawn, the floor was swept

And strewn with rushes, rosemary and may

Lay thick upon the bed on which I lay,

Where through the lattice ivy-shadows crept.

He leaned above me, thinking that I slept

And could not hear him; but I heard him say:

"Poor child, poor child": and as he turned away

Came a deep silence, and I knew he wept.

He did not touch the shroud, or raise the fold

That hid my face, or take my hand in his,

Or ruffle the smooth pillows for my head:

He did not love me living; but once dead

He pitied me; and very sweet it is

To know he still is warm though I am cold.

-Christina Rossetti

## YOU SAID IS

you said Is

there anything which

is dead or alive more beautiful

than my body,to have in your fingers

(trembling ever so little)?

Looking into

your eyes Nothing,i said,except the

air of spring smelling of never and forever.


....and through the lattice which moved as

if a hand is touched by a

hand(which

moved as though

fingers touch a girl's

breast,

lightly)

Do you believe in always, the wind

said to the rain

I am too busy with

my flowers to believe, the rain answered

-E E Cummings

www.ingramcontent.com/pod-product-compliance
Lightning Source LLC
Chambersburg PA
CBHW030914080526
44589CB00010B/302